EVERYDAY LIFE

Discover The Anglo-Saxons

EVERYDAY LIFE

Moira Butterfield

W

FRANKLIN WATTS
LONDON • SYDNEY

Franklin Watts
Published in Great Britain in 2016 by
The Watts Publishing Group

Copyright © The Watts Publishing Group 2014

Editor in chief: John C. Miles
Series editor: Sarah Ridley
Art director: Peter Scoulding
Series designer: John Christopher/White Design
Picture research: Diana Morris

Dewey number: 941.01
ISBN: 978 1 4451 3335 5

Printed in China

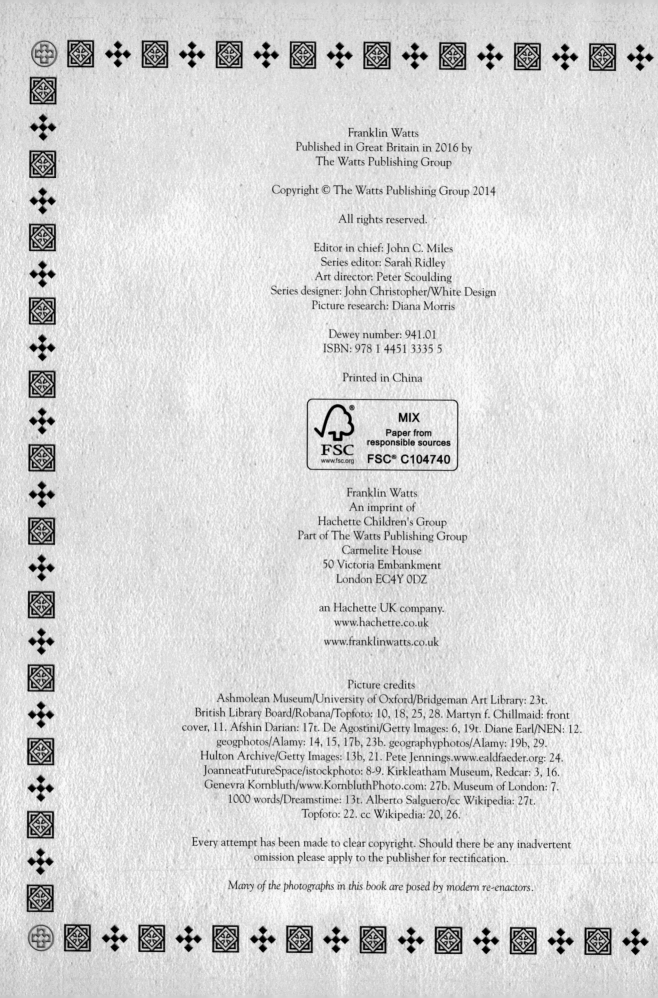

MIX
Paper from
responsible sources
FSC
www.fsc.org
FSC® C104740

Franklin Watts
An imprint of
Hachette Children's Group
Part of The Watts Publishing Group
Carmelite House
50 Victoria Embankment
London EC4Y 0DZ

an Hachette UK company.
www.hachette.co.uk

www.franklinwatts.co.uk

Picture credits
Ashmolean Museum/University of Oxford/Bridgeman Art Library: 23t.
British Library Board/Robana/Topfoto: 10, 18, 25, 28. Martyn f. Chillmaid: front
cover, 11. Afshin Darian: 17t. De Agostini/Getty Images: 6, 19t. Diane Earl/NEN: 12.
geogphotos/Alamy: 14, 15, 17b, 23b. geographyphotos/Alamy: 19b, 29.
Hulton Archive/Getty Images: 13b, 21. Pete Jennings.www.ealdfaeder.org: 24.
JoanneatFutureSpace/istockphoto: 8-9. Kirkleatham Museum, Redcar: 3, 16.
Genevra Kornbluth/www.KornbluthPhoto.com: 27b. Museum of London: 7.
1000 words/Dreamstime: 13t. Alberto Salguero/cc Wikipedia: 27t.
Topfoto: 22. cc Wikipedia: 20, 26.

Every attempt has been made to clear copyright. Should there be any inadvertent
omission please apply to the publisher for rectification.

Many of the photographs in this book are posed by modern re-enactors.

CONTENTS

MEET THE ANGLO-SAXONS

In the 400s CE new settlers arrived in southern Britain from the areas we now call Denmark, Germany and the Netherlands. They conquered south, south-west and northern England, and their leaders ruled until 1066. We call them the Anglo-Saxons.

Spearmen
The Anglo-Saxons were led by warrior-kings. This drawing from the time shows a king leading his men.

6

WARLORDS AND FARMERS

The Anglo-Saxons were led by warlords called kings. At first several kings ruled different parts of the country. Later, towards the end of Anglo-Saxon times, one king became supreme ruler. Below a king in rank came important landowners and warriors called thanes. Below the thanes came *ceorls* (pronounced 'churls'). Ceorls owned a small patch of farmland. They could become thanes if they grew rich and bought more land. Thanes and ceorls were all free men, though they were loyal to their local leader and did what he ordered.

Slave trade

Slavery was big business in Anglo-Saxon times. Slaves were sold in markets, especially in ports such as Bristol. The slaves were often exported (sold abroad). It was possible to buy yourself out of slavery, though, if you had enough money.

Whipped into line

You can see this Anglo-Saxon whip (right) at the Museum of London. It's possible it could have been used on slaves. In Anglo-Saxon law only slaves could be flogged (whipped), not free Anglo-Saxons.

BOTTOM OF THE HEAP

Below the ceorls in rank there were slaves, who were owned by somebody. People might become slaves if they were captured in war, or they might be born to slave parents. Anyone who could not pay a fine for wrongdoing, or who owed a large debt, could be forced into slavery. Sometimes poor families even had to sell their children into slavery, in return for food.

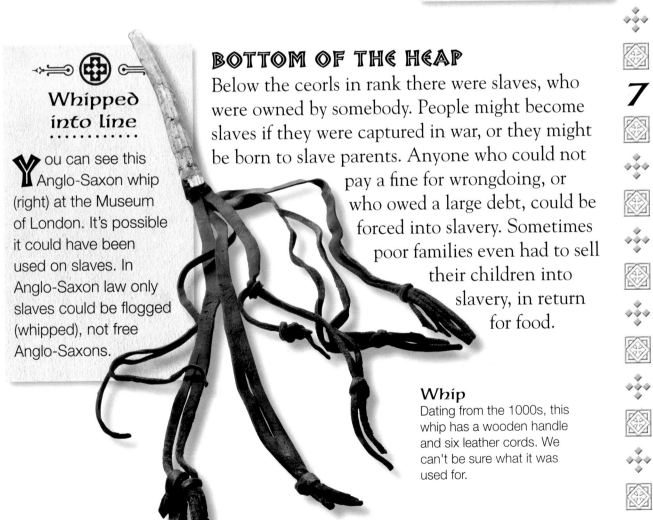

Whip
Dating from the 1000s, this whip has a wooden handle and six leather cords. We can't be sure what it was used for.

ANGLO-SAXON HOMES

Anglo-Saxons built their homes from wood, with thatch on the roof. Leaders and their warriors made their base in a big hall, while ordinary people lived in one-roomed homes in small settlements.

8

A LEADER'S HALL

A king's hall usually had other buildings around it, such as a chapel, bakery and workshops. Inside the hall the king sat on a carved chair while the rest of his warriors sat on benches or chests. They ate at long wooden tables, warmed by a blazing fire in the hearth. The walls were hung with animal skins or tapestries, helping to keep out draughts. At night everybody slept on the floor of the hall, though the king would have had his own wooden bed in a private space behind a curtain.

Not so smelly
. . . .
Anglo-Saxons rarely took baths but they did wash every day using water and soap made by mixing animal fat with wood ash. Baths were probably only for special occasions.

A FARMER'S HOME

Ordinary people lived in one-roomed homes, with a fire in a hearth but no chimney. Inside it would have been smoky and dark. At night the only light came from a candle made from a rush dipped in animal fat. Everybody lived in the same space and there might even be farm animals sharing the room, too. The floor was trampled-down earth strewn with straw, and the only pieces of furniture were a small table and stools. Wealthier people had wooden beds but poor people probably slept on the ground at night.

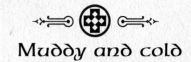

Muddy and cold

Anglo-Saxon toilets were just holes dug in the ground outside, surrounded by woven fencing for some privacy. It's thought that moss was used for wiping (paper had not yet been invented).

Go to West Stow

You can visit a reconstructed early Anglo-Saxon village at West Stow in Suffolk.

LIFE ON THE LAND

Most ordinary Anglo-Saxon people spent their days growing crops and looking after farm animals. They had to grow enough to feed themselves every year or risk starvation.

Danger in the woods

Anyone venturing away from their village had to be on their guard. The forests around settlements were not safe. There might be fierce wild boar, wolves or even murderous outlaws. Travelling away from home would have been difficult and dangerous.

FAMILY FARMERS

The fields around a village were divided into long thin strips. Each family in a settlement had their own strips of land to farm. Everything was done by hand, with the help of oxen when it was ploughing time. Families probably needed to help each other with major jobs such as ploughing and harvesting, so it was important to get on with the neighbours! Children were expected to help as soon as they were big enough. They might be given jobs such as feeding the animals.

The sowing month

This picture comes from an Anglo-Saxon calendar of the farming year. It shows men digging, flattening land and sowing seeds in March.

Everybody's busy

These re-enactors show how busy everybody must have been in an Anglo-Saxon village. Everyone had to work, including children.

GOING HUNGRY

If the weather was bad and the crops failed, everybody went hungry. Sometimes there was terrible famine. For instance, we know that a Winchester churchman called Aethelwold sold treasures from his church to feed the starving during a famine in 976. Even in a good year it was impossible to feed all the farm animals through the winter, so most of them were killed and their meat was salted or smoked to preserve it.

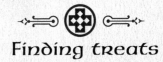

Finding treats

As well as farming, people foraged for wild food such as berries, nuts and mushrooms. They hunted wild birds and fished in the local rivers and streams. They knew when and where to look for tasty treats near their village.

GOING TO TOWN

When the Anglo-Saxons first arrived it seems they avoided the old Roman towns they found scattered across England, preferring to live in villages. Over time, however, more and more people began living in towns.

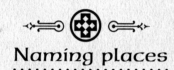

Naming places

Here are some examples of Anglo-Saxon place name endings that have survived in today's place names:

bury: a fortified settlement;
ford: a river crossing;
ham: meaning a settlement;
hurst: a wooded hill;
ton: from *tun*, meaning a village;
wick or **wich:** a farm;
worth: an enclosure.

MUDDY MARKETS

Towns grew up in places that were convenient to visit – such as a crossing place on a river, for instance. People came to buy and sell goods at the town markets, and craftspeople set up workshops to make and sell things. Anglo-Saxon towns were very small compared to modern towns, though. They consisted of just a few muddy streets lined with thatched wooden huts.

Wooden way
Town-dwellers had wooden houses lining muddy pathways.

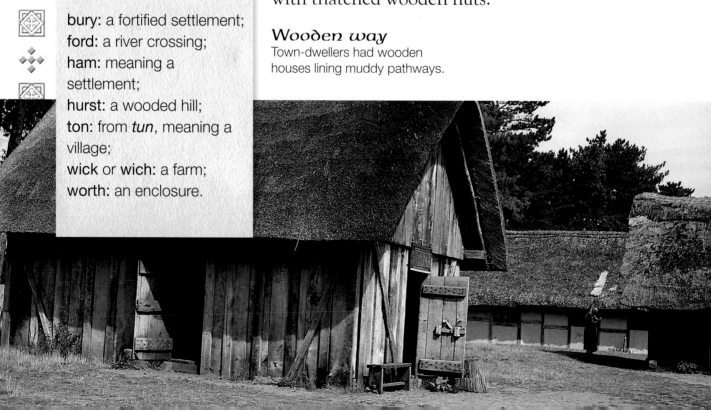

Special stones

Anglo-Saxons began to build stone churches from the 600s onwards. St Laurence's Church, Bradford-on-Avon in Wiltshire (above) is an example. Churches attracted visitors to towns.

SAFE FROM VIKINGS

In the 800s Viking raiders from Scandinavia began to attack Britain. They destroyed many villages and towns, but King Alfred of Wessex managed to stop them taking over the whole country. To help keep them out of his southern kingdom he built defensive walls and ditches around towns. He called these fortified towns *burhs*. People could have land inside a burh if they agreed to help defend it from attackers, and villagers from the countryside could find safety behind the walls if the Vikings arrived.

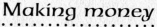

Making money

By the mid-600s the Anglo-Saxons were making silver coins for buying and selling goods. Some of these ancient coins (shown below) have been unearthed in modern towns, exactly where their owners dropped them over 1,000 years ago!

ANGLO-SAXON EATING

The food that Anglo-Saxons ate depended on their wealth and what was in season. We know about some of their meals from descriptions of feasts and from food remains that archaeologists have found.

Cutlery
People ate with their fingers or used knives and spoons.

VILLAGE EATING

Ordinary villagers ate a vegetable stew called pottage. They probably threw hunks of meat into the bubbling stew pot on special occasions. They munched on flatbread, made butter and cheese, collected birds' eggs and gathered tasty wild herbs to use in cooking. Clean fresh water was hard to find so they drank home-brewed beer or cider.

Not on the menu

Anglo-Saxons did not have some of the food we think of as normal. Sugar, potatoes, tomatoes, bananas or pineapples were not on their menu. Nor did they have oranges and lemons, but they did have apples, cherries, strawberries and other fruits that grew wild in Britain.

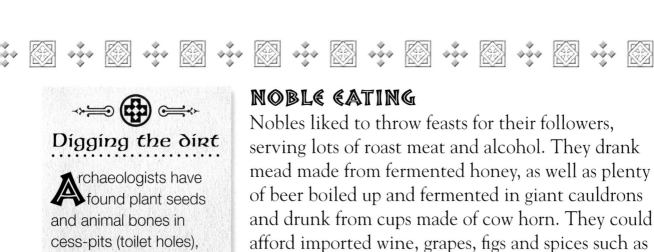

Digging the dirt

Archaeologists have found plant seeds and animal bones in cess-pits (toilet holes), telling us a little about what the Anglo-Saxons ate. The remains also tell us that they often suffered from parasites such as stomach worms. These may have entered their bodies when meat was badly-cooked and they didn't wash their hands properly before they ate.

NOBLE EATING

Nobles liked to throw feasts for their followers, serving lots of roast meat and alcohol. They drank mead made from fermented honey, as well as plenty of beer boiled up and fermented in giant cauldrons and drunk from cups made of cow horn. They could afford imported wine, grapes, figs and spices such as ginger and cinnamon. Some of the dishes would be made from creatures hunted by the noble and his men, including wild birds and boars. A feast might go on all day, sometimes even for longer.

Family food

Everything a family ate was cooked at home from ingredients they had grown or gathered themselves. Food was prepared in wooden bowls and cooked in metal pots, hung over the fire.

ANGLO-SAXON CLOTHES

Manuscript pictures and objects found in graves have given us some idea of what Anglo-Saxon people wore. Their clothing depended on how wealthy and important they were.

Beautiful bling
This gold pendant would have belonged to someone wealthy.

Hair fashion

Women covered their hair and shoulders with a veil. They probably plaited their hair or pinned it back. Men had long hair, beards and moustaches. By law, if anyone deliberately damaged a man's hair or beard he or she risked a large fine! Only slaves had shaved heads.

WOOLLY KIT

Men wore linen shirts and woollen tunics with woolly trousers or leggings wrapped round with cloth or leather strips to keep them in place. Women wore linen underdresses and woollen overdresses that looked like long pinafores. Clothing was fastened with laces or brooches and nobody wore underpants. Men and women wore belts hung with useful items such as knives and leather pouches. Nobles and churchmen wore the finest materials, such as silk.

Mystery crystal

A crystal ball about the size of a plum has been found in a number of female graves. Nobody knows what it was for, only that it usually came with a mini spoon that had holes in it like a tiny sieve. The crystal (above right) might have been used to focus the Sun's rays to light fires, or perhaps it was for a ritual.

FOUND IN THE GROUND

Jewellery such as strings of beads, finger rings and brooches have been found in Anglo-Saxon graves. Nobles owned the finest jewels, made using stones imported from faraway places such as central Europe, Russia and even Afghanistan. Beauty items have been found in graves, too, including combs made of animal bone or antlers and tiny implements such as ear-cleaning scoops and tweezers.

Women weavers

These re-enactors are showing how women often spent part of every day – spinning wool and weaving it into fabric to make clothes.

GOING TO WORK

When Anglo-Saxons first came to England they were mainly peasant farmers or warriors who fought for their local leader. Later on, when towns developed, there were lots more full-time jobs for ordinary people to do.

18

A shop on his back

Merchants imported goods and sold them at markets, but if you lived in an isolated village you might buy something from a pedlar, someone who travelled round the countryside carrying a pack full of goods to sell.

Forged in fire
A blacksmith working with metal in his forge.

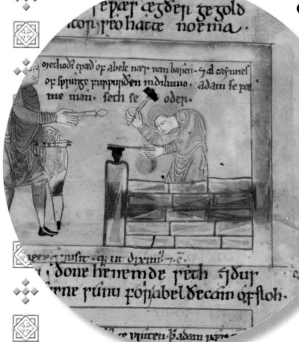

CLEVER CRAFTSPEOPLE

Blacksmiths were important Anglo-Saxon craftspeople. They made metal tools and weapons such as swords and knives, working in a forge where they heated metal in a fire and bent it into different shapes. Carpenters, potters, cobblers and jewellery-makers were also skilled workers of the time. Meanwhile weaving and sewing were craft jobs set aside for women, and it seems they were very good at it because England become known across Europe for its fine embroidery and cloth.

FARMER, MONK OR FIGHTER?

Many jobs were involved with the land – such as beekeeper, cowherd, forester, goatherd or shepherd. There were also food providers, including cheesemakers and bakers, fishermen and fowlers (wild bird hunters). Some people chose to live a religious life as a monk or a nun, devoting their days to prayer. Nobles did not need to work because they owned land and rented it out to be farmed by others. Some noblemen would have been full-time warriors.

Wood work
Anglo-Saxon craftsmen made lots of things from wood.

A religious job
Nuns, like monks, spent their days attending services, praying and working.

Name that job

Do you know someone with an Anglo-Saxon surname? Baker, Farmer, Weaver, Fisher, Fowler, Smith, Hunter and Bowyer are all examples of modern surnames that began long ago as a description of an Anglo-Saxon person's job. Bowyer comes from the word for making hunting bows.

MEN AND WOMEN

Men ruled and ran the Church at this time but a few noble women did help to rule and women ran nunneries, too. Lower ranked men and women spent their days working to feed their families.

Royal rulers
Noblewomen could try to use their influence to help their menfolk rule.

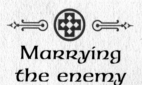

Marrying the enemy

Highborn noble women did not marry for love. They were married off in political deals between kingdoms. They might even have to be a *fricwebba* – which means 'peaceweaver'. That meant marrying into an enemy tribe or clan to help bring peace between the warring sides.

GETTING MARRIED

Women could own their own property and they had lots of legal rights. No woman could be forced to marry, for instance, and women did not have to give all they owned to their husband. When people got married, the groom made an agreement with the bride's family and paid them money. Then, on the day after the wedding, the groom gave his wife her own gift, perhaps some money or land. The word 'wedding' comes from the Anglo-Saxon word *wedd*, which means a promise.

A working partnership
In this Anglo-Saxon picture a husband digs while his wife spins wool. They are both working to provide for their families.

GETTING NAMED

Anglo-Saxons had one main name – their first name. Then they might have an added description of their job, home or their husband's name. So for example, someone might be introduced as 'Cedric the Smith', 'Baldric of Lundenwic' (London) or perhaps 'Agnes, wife of Baldric'. In late Anglo-Saxon times, some nobles began to use second names – their father's name with 'son' on the end. Some modern names that come from Anglo-Saxon times include Alfred, Aiden, Edward, Edith, Agnes, Emma and Matilda.

Wedding day traditions

At an Anglo-Saxon wedding the families met for a feast. The bride and groom wore their best clothes and the bride wore a wreath of flowers on her head. Exchanging rings, having special cakes and drinking the health of the couple are all thought to be traditions that come from this time in history.

GROWING UP

Most Anglo-Saxon children had a tough childhood of hard work, and by the age of around 12 they were considered to be adults and could marry. Their lifestyles depended on how wealthy their families were.

LEARNING FOR LIFE

Sons and daughters of farming families helped to run their homes. Girls and boys were just as important as each other, though girls were taught home skills such as weaving, sewing and brewing, while boys learnt outdoor skills such as hunting, chopping wood and ploughing. The sons and daughters of wealthy families were sometimes taught to read and write by private teachers.

Learning life
Children learnt the skills they needed from adults. Here, a re-enactor shows a child how to spin wool, Anglo-Saxon style.

Sharing children

Children from wealthy families were often fostered – sent to live with their relatives. It was thought to be good for their education and for binding families together.

TOYS AND TREASURES

Children were often buried with their favourite toys, so we know that they sometimes had wooden dolls and carved animals (especially horses) as well as toy ships and swords. They played with wooden spinning tops and musical pipes made of reeds or animal bones. We also know from child burials that children wore clothes and jewellery like their parents.

For the children

Brooches, beads and bracelets (shown here) have been found in children's graves.

Helping out

Even young children were given useful jobs to do. These children are dressed in Anglo-Saxon clothing.

Short lives

On average Anglo-Saxons died in their late-30s, though some lived far longer. Many children did not survive through to adulthood because of diseases and poor medical care. Anglo-Saxon cemeteries tend to have lots of child graves.

CATCHING CRIMINALS

There were no prisons and no police in Anglo-Saxon times. There were trials and punishments, but they were very different to those used today.

FAMILY FINES

Families were expected to seek revenge for injuries and death inflicted on their relatives. To stop terrible feuds the Anglo-Saxons brought in the payment of a *wergild*, which means 'man price'. Anyone who injured or killed somebody had to pay a fine to the victim or their family. Here are some examples of wergild from laws set in Kent in the 600s:

❖ **Broken nose** – 6 shillings;
❖ **Loss of an ear** – 12 shillings;
❖ **Loss of an eye** – 50 shillings;
❖ **Death of a slave** – 20 shillings;
❖ **Death of a freeman** – 100 shillings;
❖ **Death of a nobleman** – 300 shillings.

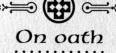

On oath

At a trial nobody examined the crime details. Instead the verdict relied mainly on how many people swore an oath (below) that the accused person was innocent. The oath of one nobleman counted for six ordinary men.

Justice done

Anglo-Saxon kings set the laws in the areas they ruled. This Anglo-Saxon picture shows a king and his advisors sitting together as a man is hanged.

GUILTY OR INNOCENT?

Local people were responsible for catching criminals in their own community. Everybody might go on a 'hue and cry' – a hunt to catch someone who had run away to avoid punishment. There would be a trial and if the verdict was 'guilty' the punishment might be a fine, mutilation (having a body part cut off), slavery or death (usually by hanging). If the court could not decide, the accused might have to go through a physical challenge called an ordeal.

Ordeals

Here are some examples of Anglo-Saxon ordeals:

By water The accused person was thrown into a river. If he floated he was guilty. If he sank he was innocent and would have to be pulled out quickly!

Ordeal by iron The accused had to hold a hot iron bar. Their burnt hand was bandaged, and then inspected after three days. If it was infected, that meant 'guilty'!

GETTING BETTER

If Anglo-Saxon people fell ill they relied on herbal remedies, healing foods and magical charms. People with knowledge of herbal cures were called leeches. One or two medical books, called leechbooks, survive from the 900s.

Who healed?

Early on in Anglo-Saxon times people would probably go to a local healer in their village - someone with knowledge of medical cures. Later on, monks and nuns became the main healers, using leechbooks to help them.

Bald's leechbook
A collection of Anglo-Saxon remedies and charms.

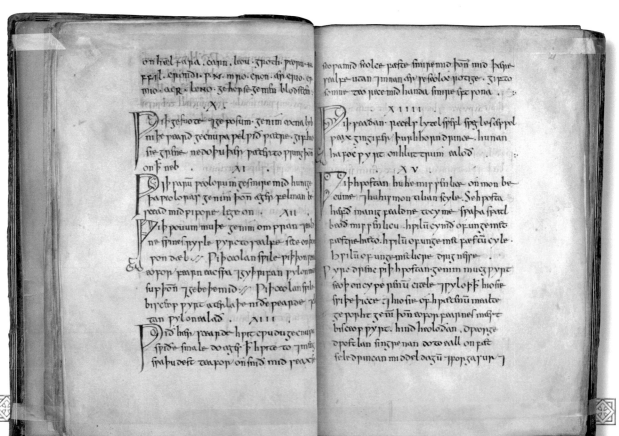

Powerful plants
Wild herbs such as burdock (right) were ground up to make medicines.

HEALING HERBS

Plants were mixed into salves (creams) or used in poultices (dressings put on wounds). Different herbs were chosen for different illnesses, and spices such as pepper and ginger were mixed in, too. Sometimes the patient was fed healing food such as broth made with specific plants and vegetables. Some of the medical ingredients sound very strange – including urine, worms and ants. But some of the plants that were used are known to be effective and are still used in medical treatments today.

Carried for luck?
This giant 4.4cm wide bead might possibly have been an amulet (a lucky object).

MAGICAL CURES

The Anglo-Saxons believed in using magic to cure illnesses, and the leechbooks contained charms to recite, as well as recipes for medicines. There were charms for all sorts of medical problems, from curing a wart to getting rid of pain, and also for getting rid of harmful enchantments thought to come from magical beings such as water-elves.

Amulets
. . . .

The Anglo-Saxons believed in carrying amulets, lucky objects that they thought would ward off illnesses and bad luck. An amulet might be a mini carved figure, a lucky stone or a religious object.

HAVING FUN

Anglo-Saxons liked to have fun! Lots of sports and games are mentioned in their manuscripts. The sports probably took place during festivals and celebrations.

Hunting
Wealthy Anglo-Saxon nobles hunted game for sport with spears or bows and arrows.

SPORTS, ANGLO-SAXON STYLE

Men took part in sports such as wrestling, tug-of-war and weightlifting with heavy rocks. They raced horses and played ball games, too. The rules of their ball games are not known, but it seems they may have used a kind of hockey stick for pushing a wooden ball along, and also hit a ball with a wooden bat, rather like baseball or cricket. They took part in swimming races and it was apparently within the rules to push other swimmers underwater!

Highborn hunting

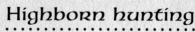

Nobles liked to go hunting as a hobby. It kept them fit and helped them practise skills they might need in battle, such as spear-throwing. Warriors would go out together in a hunting party, looking for creatures such as wild boars.

FANCY A GAME?

Anglo-Saxon boardgames had names such as *hnaftafl* and *halatafl*. The word *tafl* meant 'table' in Anglo-Saxon. Most of the boardgames that have been found used counters or round marble-shaped pieces, rather like modern backgammon or solitaire, but we don't know any of the rules for sure. If you have ever played jacks then you will recognise a game where players had to bounce a small leather ball and pick up six mini animal knucklebones between bounces. You can buy recreated Anglo-Saxon boardgames with rules that have been worked out by modern players.

I win!
Anglo-Saxon board games used counters or marble-shaped pieces, but we don't know the original rules.

Great gamblers

Lots of Anglo-Saxon gaming dice have been found, so it seems that people liked to gamble. For instance, over 50 gaming pieces made of bone and two dice made from deer antler were found in a local king's grave in Prittlewell, Essex.

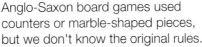

GLOSSARY

Amulet An object that is carried around because it is thought of as a lucky charm.

Anglo-Saxons People who arrived in southern Britain in the 400s CE, from the areas we now call Denmark, Germany and the Netherlands.

Brewing Making beer.

Burh An Anglo-Saxon town with a defensive wall and ditches built around it.

Cauldron A giant iron bowl used for cooking food or making beer.

Ceorl An ordinary Anglo-Saxon person who owned a small patch of land.

Cess-pit A deep hole used for toilet waste.

Famine A time when many people starve, due to crop failure.

Foraging Looking for wild food to eat, such as plants, mushrooms and berries.

Forge A blacksmith's workshop, where hot fires were used to soften metal, which was then hammered into different shapes.

Fostering When a child is looked after by another family, not their own parents.

Fricwebba An Anglo-Saxon word meaning 'peace-weaver'. Used to describe women who married into an enemy tribe or clan, to help make peace.

Hall An Anglo-Saxon leader's base, where he and his warriors lived.

Hue and cry A hunt to find somebody who had been accused of a crime and had then run away to avoid punishment.

Leech A blood-sucking animal but also the word Anglo-Saxons used to mean a healer with knowledge of medicines.

Leechbook An Anglo-Saxon book of medical cures.

Manuscript A handwritten document.

Ordeal A physical challenge meant to prove if a person was guilty of a crime or not.

ANGLO-SAXON TIMELINE

410 CE The Roman army leaves Britain.

449 The Angles and Saxons arrive by boat in south-east Britain. The Britons fight to push them back.

540 The invading Angles, Saxons and Jutes conquer England. They are pagan, not Christian.

563 Irish monk Columba founds a Christian monastery on the island of Iona.

585 By now seven separate kingdoms have formed in England – Mercia, East Anglia, Northumberland, Essex, Wessex, Sussex and Kent. Each has their own king. Over time, some kings become *bretwalda* – overlords of the other kings.

597 Aethelberht, King of Kent, becomes the first Anglo-Saxon Christian leader, converted by the monk Augustine. Gradually others convert to Christianity.

620 (approx) The death and burial of an East Anglian king (probably Redwald) at Sutton Hoo in Suffolk.

664 A meeting at Whitby decides between Celtic Christianity and the Christianity of Rome. The Christianity of Rome is preferred.

731 A monk called Bede finishes writing a history of Britain, the best source of history we have about this time.

789 The first recorded Viking attack on the British Isles, at Portland in Dorset.

793 Vikings attack the monastery at Lindisfarne.

865 A big Viking force, the Great Heathen Army, arrives and rampages across the country for the next 14 years.

Outlaw A person who is wanted for crimes, but has run away.

Pedlar Somebody who travelled round the countryside selling goods from a pack.

Pottage A vegetable stew, sometimes with meat in it.

Poultice A dressing put onto a wound. Anglo-Saxons made poultices from healing herbs.

Preserve To keep from rotting. Anglo-Saxons preserved meat and fish by smoking or salting it.

Rush light A rush (a part of a plant) dipped in animal fat and burned like a candle.

Strip farming When a field is divided into strips and each strip is farmed separately.

Thane An Anglo-Saxon warrior and wealthy landowner.

Thatch A roof made of dry plant material such as straw or rushes.

Vikings Raiders who arrived from Scandinavia in the 800s.

Wergild A fine paid to a victim or the victim's family to compensate for an injury or death.

WEBLINKS

Here are some websites with information about the Anglo-Saxons.

http://www.weststow.org/
The reconstructed Anglo-Saxon village of West Stow.

www.britishmuseum.org
Search for Anglo-Saxons on this giant site full of treasures.

http://www.regia.org/pastimes. htm
Find out about Anglo-Saxon sports and games.

http://www.battle1066.com
All about the Battle of Hastings in 1066.

http://www.show.me.uk/tag/ Anglo-Saxon
Anglo-Saxon themed games and online activities from museums around the country.

31

878 Alfred, King of Wessex, defeats Danish Vikings at the Battle of Edington. The Danes and the Anglo-Saxons agree the Treaty of Wedmore, splitting England between them.

899 Alfred dies. He is succeeded as King of Wessex by his son, Edward.

911 Alfred's daughter Aethelflaed takes over the rule of Mercia after the death of her husband.

937 Athelstan, King of Wessex and Mercia, defeats an army of Vikings and Scots at the Battle of Brunanburh. He then rules over the whole of England.

1016 Danish King Cnut becomes King of England, deposing Ethelred the Unready. Anglo-Danish kings rule England for a while.

1042 Edward, son of Ethelred the Unready, takes power. Brought up in Normandy, he apparently promised his throne to his great-nephew, William, when he died.

1066 Harold Godwinson is chosen as king but reigns for only ten months. The Anglo-Saxons are defeated by William, Duke of Normandy, at the Battle of Hastings.

Note to parents and teachers

Every effort has been made by the Publishers to ensure that the web sites in this book are suitable for children, that they are of the highest educational value, and that they contain no inappropriate or offensive material. However, because of the nature of the Internet, it is impossible to guarantee that the contents of these sites will not be altered. We strongly advise that Internet access is supervised by a responsible adult.

INDEX